The Mental Scars Brought to Light

Laura Gorman

Copyright © Laura Gorman 2024

All Rights Reserved

No part of this publication may be reproduced, stored in a retrieval system, or transmitted in any form or by any means, electronic, mechanical, photocopying, recording, or otherwise, without the written permission of the author or the publisher.

Contents

Dedication	i
Acknowledgments	ii
About the Author	iii
Introduction	1
Behind the Mask	3
Little Wings	4
The Four Shadows	5
Darkness Into Light	6
Behind The Uniform	7
Memories Upon Your Face	9
Battleground of Life	10
Time Waits for No Man	11
Premature Gift	12
What She Will Never Have	13
365	14
Her Body, Her Choice	15
Depress the Stigma	16
The Path Travelled	17
Drowning In a Sea of Darkness	18
2023	19
Before You Go	20
Always and Never	21
No Filter	22
Unbroken Souls	23
When Your Mind Is a Prison	24
Second Chances	25
I've Gone Fishing	26
Unspoken	27
Let Her	28
Message Delivered	29
Lessons	30
In The Deep End	31
Give Heaven Hell	32
The Demons in the Bottle	33
More Than a Statistic	34
Define Love	35
Flowers	36
The Cancer Grew	37
Subconscious Stitches	38
The Angel on MY Shoulder	39

Dedication

This book is simply a dedication to those people who have stood by my side. To those who have been there when I needed them. To those whom I have shared many adventures and laughs with.

Here's to having many more shared memories with those who truly matter most.

Acknowledgments

About the Author

Laura Gorman hails from the quaint and historic village of Ballinamuck, nestled in the heart of Ireland. At the age of twenty-one, fueled by a passion for service and an unwavering dedication to making a difference, Laura made the bold decision to relocate to Northampton, England. It was here that she started focusing on her career journey in the ambulance service, specifically with the esteemed East Midlands Ambulance Service.

Through her experiences on the front lines of emergency response, Laura's eyes were opened wide to the myriad struggles and complexities of the modern world. Her journey, marked by compassion, resilience, and a deep understanding of human connection, has inspired her to pen a collection of poignant poems. These verses encapsulate not only her personal experiences but also the trials faced by her friends, family, and colleagues in the demanding realm of emergency services.

Laura's writing is a testament to the strength found in vulnerability, the power of empathy, and the beauty of resilience in the face of adversity. Her words resonate with authenticity and offer solace to those navigating their own paths through life's challenges. In each poem, readers will discover a heartfelt narrative woven with compassion and insight, inviting them to reflect on the shared experiences that unite us all.

"Death leaves a heartache no one can heal; Love leaves a memory no one can steal."

-Richard Puz.

Introduction

This is my second book being published, following my first book The Mental Scars You Cannot See. This book focuses on life growing up in your twenties and trying to find your path in life. It's about making mistakes, watching people you love aging, dealing with loss, trying to cope with life's stresses and trying to navigate relationships with people.

Often in today's society, we get too caught up in everything that we have to do and not focus on the here and now. If you just take a minute to look around, at the simple things in life, and look at how many things in life we cannot change. Often, the things we stress and worry about in life are very similar to this. We cannot change them, so why do we spend so much of our time stressing about them?

With saying this, it is also vital that we do not take these things for granted. We have emotions for a reason, and they must be listened to. If something was going to attack you, you would go into 'Fight or Flight mode.' This is our brain's way of telling us we need to react to something that is going to harm us. Our emotions are the same as this: if you are starting to feel overwhelmed with life or everyday struggles, then you need to listen to your body. You need to react in a way that best suits you. This could be by removing yourself from a situation, taking the time to process your thoughts, talking with some friends or family etc. The best things in life are often the simplest things. They come without a price tag. You just need to open your eyes, and you'll find them.

I would never tell anyone the reasons or story behind why a poem was written for the reason- I view poetry very similarly to how I view music. If you were to listen to the exact same song as me, we could both feel completely differently about the meaning at the end. It may trigger a happy memory for me, whereas it may trigger something upsetting or dramatic for you. Poetry is the same. It's for the reader to come up with their own conclusion and what is related to them, not for the author to tell the reader what it's about. Otherwise, the words written have no life. It's for you, the reader, to give them meaning.

Behind the Mask

If people only knew you were constantly wearing a mask,
How many people, then, would have stopped you to ask,
If we're really doing ok, behind the face in which you paint,
Or would they say, well, you got on with life without a single complaint.

If people only knew you were constantly so sad inside,
And when you were all alone, you just sat there and cried,
You would apologise for the days in which the mask slipped,
And tell everyone how great things were as if you had read it from a script.

If people only knew you were constantly in pain,
How many people would have stopped to hear you explain,
That your life was slowly slipping away, out of your control,
There was only one thing on your mind, it was your final goal.

If people only knew you were constantly just not ready to talk,
How many people would come up to you and not just continue to walk,
Sometimes, the people with the hardest shells are the ones who are truly broken,
Now it's time to make sure people talk and leave nothing left unspoken.

Little Wings

There are days I sit here and imagine your little face,
It seems some people, are too precious for earth and never got a place.
I imagine you in my arms as you dance your chubby feet,
It seems heaven needed another angel, so we never got to meet.

So if there is a god, then someone please tell me why,
How could he let such an innocent and pure little one die?
I never got a chance to meet you or even give you a name,
I want you to know I think of you every day, and my life won't be the same.

To the angels who were never born or quickly gained their wings,
Know you are in our thoughts through everything life brings.

I know your life was inevitably too short, but you are on my mind every day,
I will live my life in your memory, as you were just too precious to stay.

The Four Shadows

Before she knew it, there were four shadows there,
Even lurking behind her, when she was unaware,
As the time quickly passed, the shadows grew even greater,
In the blink of an eye, four shadows weren't there later.

There was a time that the shadows were always around,
Now, as time has passed, they are nowhere to be found,
She misses the times that they would get under her feet,
As when they were around, her life felt complete.

The shadows now visit with shadows of their own,
They are a reminder of how quickly time has flown,
She wished she'd made the most of her shadows, as they were a reminder,
That one day, she'll look back, and they won't be behind her.

Darkness Into Light

If you ever lose yourself, out in the dark unknown,
I want you to know that you will never be alone.
For I will be your lighthouse when all seems lost,
You will see the light again, at whatever cost.

I will shine the brightest light to guide you back home,
Lead you to the right path when your mind does roam.
As when in the darkness, we need someone to hold the torch,
To leave the light on to guide you, or be sat waiting on the porch.

Know you are not in this dark place, just by yourself,
Like no man ever won a war entirely by himself.
So know when you lose yourself, out in the dark,
I'll be right by your side to reignite your spark.

Behind The Uniform

Know behind the uniform in which we wear,
Is someone who joined the job because we care,
For the times you call us in the middle of the night,
Because your loved one has given up the fight.

Most people will never be able to understand,
What its like to sit with those dying, as you hold their hand,
And when we are finished, we go to the next call,
As if what just happened never happened at all.

We'll walk into strangers homes like we've been there before,
Without knowing what's before us or what's behind the door,
We'll be there for you every day of the year,
Even on the days, we can't be with those we hold dear.

Screams we remember after telling you your loved one has died,
When we close our eyes, we still see you laying by their side,
The uniform does not protect us from the things we observe,
But when we're with you, our own emotions we'll reserve.

We don't do it for the thanks or certainly not for the pay,
We do it to help strangers loved ones stay another day,
And when a heart stops beating and we're too late,
Know it breaks us, and we carry that weight.

Know behind the uniform, we're just like you,
Trying to navigate our lives and make it through,
When you see us at the end of the day, as we sit there and cry,
Know we gave our all and our very best we did try.

Memories Upon Your Face

The lines on our faces, are to remind us of our story,
Every mark, bruise and grey hair, in all its glory.
You are still the better half of me, even after all these years,
As I look to you now, with my eyes full of tears.

Your eyes are still the ones in love that I once fell,
The ones I look to with any worries, I know I can tell.
Yours is the hand I will hold until your last breath,
Know I will be by your side until your sorrowful death.

The lines on our faces are an aid for us to remember,
Our children, grandchildren and every family member.
My darling wife, take a look around at the amazing family that we raised,
The love here for you could never be put into words, or enough gratitude praised.

On the day you close your eyes for the final time,
Know to get back to you, any mountain, I would climb.
As my love for you, I promise to take with me to the ground,
As a love like ours, never again could it ever be found.

Battleground of Life

When we were young, we couldn't wait to grow older,
Now, the world is our battleground and our role is a soldier.
Meanwhile, we sit in the trenches, and the world has us in their aim,
To protect you and make it home, I'd walk through any flame.

I know we'll carry each other right to the end of the line,
But know to protect you, I would jump upon any mine.
Know I would even carry you upon my broken back,
Even when the rest of the world, has us in their attack.

Know I'd be your lifeboat if you were to ever drown at sea,
As a life without you by my side, I could never possibly foresee.
We don't share the same blood, but you'll always be my brother,
You're the one I chose to battle with, there will never be another.

Time Waits for No Man

The measurement of a man's success is not what's in his bank,
Or the status he holds in society, at any given rank,
It's what the people at home think, the ones who know him true,
And, when he looks in the mirror at the person that he can view.

A real man's strength is really measured in his actions,
When people at home need him, it's the measurement of his reactions,
It's the man who can swallow his pride and reap in the sorrow,
He is the man who will be even more successful today and tomorrow.

When he gets home and looks in the mirror at the person staring back,
He knows his family is by his side, and his emotions he can unpack,
He will be the man that little boy's eyes once wanted him to be,
Then he'll know that whatever time he has left, his conscience can be free.

Premature Gift

This little dot born before your time,
You were not ready for the world, in your prime,
A defenseless and delicate little creature,
The doctor proclaimed; he's calling a preacher.

There were days I could only peer through the glass,
The nurses told me these days, too, will pass,
And one day, I will be able to hold you again,
But that I also have to build my own strength for then.

You were stronger than anyone really knew,
Even on the days that you turned blue,
Everyday slowly, more you grew,
Then the nurses said, I could finally hold you.

For such a little one, you never give up the fight,
Promise you will do the same for me tonight,
Know, in the morning, I will be back with you there,
For now, I leave you in the walking angel's care.

What She Will Never Have

If I leave this world too soon, I just need you to know,
My love for you, she will never be able to show.
She can have everything that I once owned,
As I'm afraid, my love for you can never be cloned.

She can have my house, car and all my stuff,
As the love I have for you, will always be enough.
On the day I said I do, I meant it to our last day,
Make sure she knows our love never goes away.

I wish for nothing more than for us to grow old,
But if, before my time, my heart should suddenly go cold.
Make sure she knows she can never replicate my love,
As that for you, will still shine brighter even from above.

365

Some things that we love don't always last,
As it now shows, another 365 days have now past,
Where you are, or your stories, I no longer know,
It seemed together, as two, we could no longer grow.

Time has kept ticking, just like you said it would,
The many good times we had, have I just misunderstood,
I thought when 365 had passed, you'd make your way back home,
Instead, it feels like your heart has only decided to roam.

Today should have been the day that I bought you a card,
To remember another 365, instead, there has been no regard,
Instead, it's just another day with nothing to celebrate,
Now I sit here for another 365, I know will have to wait.

Her Body, Her Choice

Tell a woman what she can do with her body, who do you think you are?
Are you going to sit with her and mend her body from the eternal scar,
Her mind already in turmoil, without you telling her what she must choose,
Her body is not yours to use and abuse with your religious and political views.

You try and strip a woman of her own body and ability for her to choose,
You try break her down slowly and control her actions, but she'll refuse,
She'll make her decision on her own situation and what's truly best,
So, stand out with your signs, her decision won't change because of your protest.

Do you believe she has not tried to think of every possibility,
So, what she decides to do with her body is her responsibility,
Don't try and tell her she is going to hell, for when she chooses to take action,
A woman's body used to take away from your sad life, just using her as a distraction.

Depress the Stigma

If only he knew his answers were not at the end of a rope,
Life's worries and problems, he just could no longer cope,
If only he had spoken to a family member or a friend,
He'd have seen many more happy memories he was meant to spend.

Depression does not respect personal boundaries or space,
It can unawarely attack a person at any time or place,
He would then sit in a dark room, and every decision question why?
Everything he now does is wrong, and he'll just sit there and cry.

So, when you question why he left you on this earth too soon,
Know, he battled every single day to make the next afternoon,
Depression does not strike lightly or is even a bit forgiving,
Just remember the world's a better place when you are still living.

The Path Travelled

I know that everything may currently seem lost,
Just know that you will find your way at any cost.
If you were coming up to a fork in the road,
How far would you travel before you slowed.
Would you first ensure you had all the details,
Or, just take a path without knowing what it entails.

Some roads people take may only be uphill,
This is when you have to show all your strength and will.
Some roads we take may have many twists and turns,
This can be the journey where some of us best learns.
When you decide on the path that best suits you,
Know the hardship is worth it, at the end, and projects the best view.

If you had taken a moment, stood there at the fork in the road,
Look as far as you can to see what each path showed.
Then, you can view what road best suits your own ability,
Check all the hidden bumps and hills for their stability.
You will then know what's needed to travel without taking a hit,
It's when the road feels like the hardest path that you must not quit.

Drowning In a Sea of Darkness

Drowning in a sea of darkness, I could no longer see the light,
With every breath to the end, I promise I tried to fight.
The waves slowly got higher, I tried to vigorously battle through,
Know, at the very end, my thoughts were only that of you.

There were moments I managed to hold my head just above the water,
Even then, I was feeling suffocated, and my mind was for the slaughter.
I did not have the strength to keep myself afloat as my lungs filled,
Know, in those final moments, my mind and soul were finally stilled.

I took one final look out to the horizon and the clear sky,
This was when I knew it was truly my time to say goodbye.
Know my mind can now rest, as the worries have been taken away,
I will still be looking out for you from afar every single day.

2023

As 2023 came to an end,
We remembered the events along the way,
Finally time with loved ones, we could spend,
Reminiscing the folks we lost, who couldn't stay.

Full of ups and downs throughout the year,
Many laughs and tears, with those dear,
The important things were made very clear,
Embrace, make memories with the people near.

As a new chapter begins today,
Don't let your mind go wandering astray,
Tomorrow's just another day,
We'll figure the rest out along the way.

Before You Go

Why am I still looking over my shoulder,
It was you, not me, that decided to hold her.
Why do I feel like I've done something wrong,
I was sat here, waiting at home all along.

There's something about you beside me here,
Has made all my feelings just disappear.
You said you were staying with some friends,
Well, now, this is where our story ends.

All along, through your teeth, you lied,
Stronger together and a future, you implied.
But you took her to the bed that I made,
Our future together, you have now betrayed.

I went through the trouble to keep her eyes dry,
Now I'm lost, and you don't even care if I cry.
You lied to my face, and now you lie with her,
My soulmate, at least, I thought you were.

I should be moving on, and you should be long gone,
What stands in the way, my love for you has never withdrawn.
How could you tell me you still love me but walk out the door,
Now, my mind is a battlefield, and my heart is at war.

So, just tell me that you never loved me and just break my heart,
Make your last words ice cold so I can hate you before you part.
Please shatter my heart into a million pieces on the ground,
At least then, I wouldn't still be waiting and wanting you around.

Always and Never

Always the one who got away,
Always the one who couldn't stay,
It doesn't matter who comes after you,
They will never compare, to us two.

Always going to be my closest friend,
Anyone who came between, I'll defend.
Too scared to ask for a second chance,
But no one comes close, never mind romance.

You will forever be the one who got away,
Not a day has passed that I didn't pray,
You'd come back to where I thought we belonged,
Now, the pain everyday has been prolonged.

Turns out always doesn't last forever,
I hope you're happy now, however,
But just know, since we decided to part,
There has only been a void in my heart.

No Filter

The memories you try capture through the lens,
Trying to keep up with the latest trends.
Eyes are down, and fingers briskly clicking,
The best angles and filters you'll be picking.

If you just look up and take in what's around,
This is where the real memories can be found.
The feeling of the wind and sun beaming on the cliffs,
The real beauties can be seen and all life's natural gifts.

Live your life for the moments that are here now,
Give yourself time, the real beauties you should allow,
To keep in their natural and pure state,
This is when you'll see, more people can relate.

Unbroken Souls

Know I can't say goodbye,
As to me, you will never die.
I will just look up to the sky,
Asking God why he let you fly.

Just another day is all I need,
To ask God why he's full of greed.
To have you back, I tried to plead,
With my request, he disagreed.

He told me that you were happy there,
And you were sat upon the highest chair.
No more pain or worries, you had to bear,
Your broken soul, he has worked to repair.

He told me that we could never be apart,
As I just had to look deep into my heart.
That is where will be, your forever home,
I now know that I will never be alone.

When Your Mind Is a Prison

*Your voice will always be heard,
You just need to say the word.
I know you've been in this place before,
But you are not alone anymore.*

*I have served my own sentence, alone in the dark,
I know it only takes one person's remark,
To send you back to that depressing prison,
And then again, the devil has risen.*

*When he steals your mind, of all its reasoning,
Your spirit and body has begun weakening,
When you feel like you can no longer make it through,
I will break you out as we deter the screw.*

Second Chances

I wish I never knew what it was like to love you,
As the day you left, my heart split in two.
I then wouldn't miss what I didn't know,
What it felt to love someone as I watched you grow.

The hand that always fit perfectly in mine,
As two different worlds, we were able to combine.
You will always remain my missing part,
A place for you, forever reserved in my heart.

I will understand if you have to start anew,
I just need you to know before you do.
If, in another life, we got a second chance,
I would seize it without even taking a glance.

I've Gone Fishing

To escape the world, it's the place I go,
When I'm here, time only moves slow.
When I need to escape from all sound,
This is the place that I can be found.

When it's time to go and clear my head,
When I need to put my worries to bed.
I sit here listening to the birds in the tree,
It's the place I know my mind can be free.

The outside world, I'm now able to shut out,
Not a care for if, I only catch trout.
It's being sat here, amongst nature and the lake,
From life's stresses, I can now take a break.

The pressures of the world just swim away,
A smile on my face the only thing I display.
It's the place I go for some quiet and space,
If you're looking for me, I'm at my happy place.

Unspoken

One night, where I thought I was all on my own,
I heard a voice calling that I was no longer alone,
He said through the darkness that my work was now done,
As my time to rest and recover had now begun.

I told him I was not worthy, for I had sinned,
He told me this didn't mean my light had dimmed,
I was to pack up my stuff and leave right away,
But I told him I still had many things that I needed to say.

There were still many thoughts stored away in my head,
I'm sorry, but I just cannot leave them unsaid,
He told me my path to salvation, he had made clear,
But my words unspoken, I could not just leave here.

I stepped away from him, as I then began to cry,
I now had a second chance, and I had to give it a try,
I now know when the time comes again to take his hand,
All the words I have to say will remain here on land.

Let Her

I couldn't imagine my life without you in it,
As you had given life a new meaning, I must admit,
Your eyes were the ones who had given mine a new life,
With you around, there was no reason for any strife.

As when I felt like nobody else was there,
I thought you were the answers to my prayer,
When I felt no one else would really care,
You showed me there was no reason to be in despair,
When I was broken into tiny pieces on the ground,
You told me that I now had been found.

I would have sat up with you all night,
And showed you, for us, there was a reason to fight,
Why am I the only one trying to make this work,
While you sit there and just snigger and smirk,
Now you tell me it'd be better if I was just a friend,
Why has it taken for you to tell me right to the very end.

You will now talk shit about me behind my back, it makes no sense,
When I'm not there to defend my side, you'll laugh at my expense,
So, was I just your toy to use until you found someone better,
Well, if she too wants to be disappointed, then go ahead let her.

Message Delivered

I am awoken by my phone, as my screen shines bright,
As my eyes peal open, the only time they shine with delight,
For your name was upon my screen, the only time my eyes dilated,
This was the one time, through my eyes, you could see I was elated,
For the person who was upon my screen, we could never be more than friends,
But I hope today won't be the day you tell me our story ends.

I sit up on the sofa and put a pillow behind my head,
Before I could open your message, I heard him calling me to bed,
The voice I heard was not the one I wanted; it should have been you there,
So, I told him to go back to sleep, and I was to rest here on the chair,
I looked back through your messages to see where we went wrong,
As maybe we could fix it, and we'd be back where we belong.

There are times I wish I could be a passenger in your brain,
Then maybe I could understand how it is you drive me insane,
If I was to write my story again, you would be my main character at home,
But now we're in different places, not by ourselves but still alone,
I always wondered if I told you how I really felt, would things have changed,
Now, it feels like the one who knew me most has suddenly been estranged.

I'm afraid to open your message, as I don't know what it is you have to say,
As I know once I've opened it, everything we have might go away,
So, I will wait until the morning to find out what is our fate,
Then, to tell you how I really feel, it may not be too late.

Lessons

One day, it will just click that you still have a lot to learn,
To those older and wiser, we must listen, as one day it will be our turn,
When you think people are nagging you or trying to get on your back,
Realize they are trying to teach you the knowledge in which you lack.

There are still many things in which we younger don't know,
Many mistakes and failed attempts that we must undergo,
This is where the important lessons are to be learnt,
And, if you don't listen hard enough, in the end, you will get burnt.

It's not because older people are always proven right,
But they have also chosen wrong and then had to fight,
So, if you listen hard enough and don't make the same mistakes,
Then your life may be much easier, and you'll have less heartaches.

In The Deep End

I'm so tired of being thrown in the deep end,
My thoughts and my actions I have to defend,
Surely, there's an easier way than always fighting,
This isn't the life you promised, that you said was exciting.

This is when you said I wouldn't sink but swim,
But instead, I'm fighting for life and limb,
Why does everything just feel so hard,
The easy life you must have on guard.

When you're ready, dial down the difficulty setting,
There must be a button that you're forgetting,
If you could hurry up, my patience is wearing thin,
I'm ready now for my life to begin.

Give Heaven Hell

The day you left through the church doors for the final time,
Up to the angels, you decided, you had to go and climb.
Did you see, there were people cued out all three doors,
Even though outside, the heavens opened as it pours.

Can you believe you finally got your son in a suit and tie,
Like you, he cleared the pub out beforehand so he wouldn't cry.
My friend, I hope you're still racing through every street,
Making sure you have many more stories for when again we meet.

From the man upstairs, I hope you're hiding your cans and your white,
And you're still partying right through to the end of night.
Making them wonder how you even got a place at the pearly gates,
While you're perched against them, laughing with all your mates.

When the man upstairs realises you're not ready to be there,
Tell him I'll have a word and our war stories we can compare.
Just like your time on earth, continue to give them hell,
But for now, my friend, I'll say a final farewell.

The Demons in the Bottle

I tried to drown my demons, but it turns out they can swim,
They must have recently enlisted or have been going to the gym.
As this time, they've really hit me harder than ever before,
They have come for more than vengeance, they are here for a war.

The more I try and drown them, the louder they become,
They will not stop at nothing until they've turned me numb.
Even on the days to their demands, I try and surrender,
They ensure the agony and pain I will always remember.

I tried to drown my demons, but they continue to come out at night,
As soon as it becomes quiet, and I turn out the light.
They ensure never again will I be able to have any peace,
But it turns out trying to drown them, has made their presence increase.

More Than a Statistic

They are more than just a statistic on your screen,
They are a reminder of the lives that should have been,
Many more years they could have had on earth,
If only they knew how much they would be missed and their worth.

One day, they were here, and the next day, they were gone,
They could no longer see a way to carry on,
No one could truly see the amount of torment they had to bear,
To hide their true feeling daily and keep you unaware.

There are real people and families behind the figures you read,
It's time the government started to realise and take heed,
The figures of suicides should not still be climbing,
The time for change is now, there will not be a better timing.

Define Love

To fall in love is the act of faith and trust,
It's what other people believe and what we hear them discuss,
To give someone else full transparency and control,
But the definition of love, do we know it as a whole?

In love and madness, you can find some sanity,
It is often defined with words of profanity,
It can remain very mysterious without a definition,
To find it and its meaning remains everyone's mission.

How can we love someone else if we don't know who we are,
The act of love, I have always found very bizarre,
If you can only view yourself through looking in a mirror,
How can we learn about something we can't see more clearer.

They say you have to love yourself before you love another,
How can you do this if your only view is that of others,
What other people see is what you define as I,
So does that mean your definition of love is only through another's eye.

Flowers

I'm convinced I'll never be the girl that gets the flowers,
As it turns out, I actually have superpowers,
To find all the boys who want to lie and cheat,
Then again, my relationship status I have to delete.

I'm convinced I'll never be the girl that gets the flowers,
Instead, I'll sit in my own company here for hours,
Wondering where it is that I keep going wrong,
And questioning is it something I've been doing all along.

I'm convinced I'll never be the girl that gets the flowers,
But being strong on your own it surely empowers,
To make sure you're comfortable in your skin,
And the feelings in which you hold within.

So it's ok, don't worry, I'll buy my own flowers,
Everything I work for is now mine, not ours,
Turns out it's better being able to grow on your own,
And you can be much happier, even when you're alone.

The Cancer Grew

*I'm sorry I had to leave, but the cancer grew,
I had to go north, and it was time I flew,
So hold your dad even tighter for me tonight,
Tell him, with ye there, it will all be alright.*

*I promise heaven is not all that far away,
You can still talk to me, and I will hear what you have to say,
Just look up to the sky and know I'm there,
And when you close your eyes, know I'm in the air.*

*I know you slowly had to watch my life slip by,
But darling, it breaks me to see you cry.
Know, I am no longer suffering or in any pain,
And the love I have for you, words could never explain.*

Subconscious Stitches

The voices in her head zoom from ear to ear,
She just prays that no one else can hear,
The insane things that they try and tell her to do,
She just hopes that you can't hear them, too.

She fears that when others are around,
That a word might slip, and they find it profound,
So she'll sew her lips together, as tight as she can,
To keep the words inside, was always the plan.

The hairs on her arms stand to attention,
And her shoulders rise under the tension,
Her breathing becomes quicker, and her heart races,
When she looks around and sees so many faces.

Then, the air becomes thicker and harder to find,
And the voices become louder in her mind,
She wants to race out the door as quick as she can,
As being around people, the voices were not a fan.

Fear flows through her veins, making her ice cold,
But the voices inside couldn't be controlled,
They will tell her she's not good enough and she doesn't belong,
But she was determined that she had to prove the voices wrong.

She sits there slowly pealing away the stitches,
And takes a deep breath as her mind switches,
When those she feels comfortable with are beside her there,
The voices could be silenced, and her thoughts she can share.

The Angel on MY Shoulder

Most days, we spent shouting up the stairs, as we would quarrel and bicker,
Then suddenly, in the haze of time, there was just quiet as you grew sicker,
I could see your spirit slowly fading from your eyes as I held you even tighter,
I would have done anything to give you my spirit and again see that little fighter,
Everyday your body was becoming frail, as I could see you getting weaker,
The future we had planned, with you still with us, was becoming bleaker.

I'd give anything just to have five more minutes, with you beside me here,
Even if it was to have another argument, I just need the sound of your voice to be near,
For your smile could light up an entire room, even in the darkness that it currently shows,
Our family has been torn apart, and the tears are like the river that continuously flows.

There is now a chilling breeze as I sit here, is it you upon my shoulder?
It should have been you sitting here, that was now growing older,
But you taught me the act of strength and courage just before you left,
As without it, to carry on with our lives, how could I after your death.

I'd give anything to hear your voice again, just one final time,
Now, I sit here alone in the pew and hear the church bells as they chime,
I know the angels finally found you there, sleeping at their gate,
As the pain you had to carry on earth was becoming overweight,
My little one, I will continue to tell you everyday, just how much I love you,
Until you take my hand again at the gates, and together, we can walk through.

www.ingramcontent.com/pod-product-compliance
Lightning Source LLC
Chambersburg PA
CBHW070340120526
44590CB00017B/2958